flowers
from
God

Enjoy teaching
for Jesus.

Marlene LeFever

Dedicated to Sunday school teachers
who demonstrate Jesus' love
to this generation.

flowers from God

Thank-You Notes for Sunday School Teachers

Marlene LeFever

NEXGEN
Building the New Generation of Believers

An Imprint of Cook Communications Ministries
Colorado Springs, Colorado

Cook Communications Ministries, Colorado Springs, Colorado 80918
Cook Communications, Paris, Ontario
Kingsway Communications, Eastbourne, England

Editor: John Conaway
Designer: Pat Miller
Front Cover Design: S. Ann Harjes
Cover Photography: Photodisc, Inc.

First Printing, 2002. Printed in Korea.
2 3 4 5 6 7 8 9 10 Printing / 07 06 05 04 03

ISBN: 0781438918

Library of Congress Cataloging-in-Publication Data
CIP data applied for.

CONTENTS

FLOWERS FROM GOD

I got home late from work and that made me late for teacher training meeting. Was teaching Sunday school really worth all this hassle? My commitment felt never ending and not all that significant. I was exhausted.

I grabbed my mail, dashed out to my car, and predictably got stopped at the longest red light in town. I fumed as I shuffled through my mail: bills, "to occupant," and one letter with a return address I didn't recognize. I ripped it open.

> *Dear Marlene,*
>
> *You probably don't remember me, but years ago you were my Bible teacher. Thank you for teaching me about Jesus. Thank you for making me feel as if I could survive that difficult year, that I might be someone God loved.*
>
> *That was the year I decided I would give Jesus my life. You played a big part in my decision.*
>
> *I'm now a pastor's wife and a mother, but more important to you, I suspect, is that I'm also a Sunday school teacher!*

The light changed, and so had my attitude. It was as if God had sent me a bouquet of flowers, and He had chosen the perfect evening to deliver them. I could hardly wait until the next red light to "smell" them again. The letter continued with phrases that God knew I needed to hear: "You made a difference . . ." "I watched your life and . . ." "You helped me think through . . ."

Flowers from God! I get them. You get them. Every volunteer whose story is told in this book gets them. But sometimes we're too busy to realize that flowers have arrived. We miss the precious moments in the Sunday rush to get the puppets out and the paste put away and the potty breaks in before it's really too late and the answer given to that question we weren't prepared for and . . .

There is no greater calling than teacher, no more important job in the church. This book celebrates Christian education volunteers like you and like me.

May God use these stories of real teachers to make us more aware of the flowers He wants us to receive.

On-Time Flowers

Montgomery, Alabama. God planted the seeds for flowers He knew Marsha would need over four decades before she actually received them.

In the worst week of her ministry, three of her faithful teachers died. One mother died in a swimming accident. She was the teacher who volunteered to clean the bathrooms after VBS because, she said, "That job won't get many takers." Another mother died of cancer much sooner than anyone expected. A father died in a car crash.

Marsha said, "I just put my head down and cried, 'Lord, I quit. I can't direct this ministry. It hurts too much.' To my surprise, God guided me to my childhood Bible. It's an inexpensive white children's Bible that I still keep on my shelf as a reminder of why I work with children today. I opened the Bible and there on the first few pages were verses written in my fifth-grade handwriting—the exact verses of encouragement I needed that very day.

"I remembered that in 1955 my Sunday school teacher had suggested I write them in the front of my Bible because I might need them someday. That day came decades later. Those verses were God's direct message to me: 'Keep serving Me, no matter what.'"

Rock Flowers

Los Angeles. Lanie didn't know how to be a parent. She had grown up in an abusive home and her parents were never around. At sixteen, she was thrown out. Through a series of miracles, she ended up in college, met Christ, and married a Christian man. This is Lanie's bouquet to her daughter's preschool Sunday school teacher:

> When I became a parent, I was totally unprepared. I'd never seen good parenting and had no idea how to help my daughter understand about Jesus. So when a friend suggested my two-year-old Amy should be in Sunday school, I enrolled her. If that's what good parents did, I'd do it.

One day I overheard Amy singing, "The wise man built his house upon the rock." She sang that one line over and over and over because it was the only line she remembered.

"Mommy," she finally asked me, "what comes after rock?" I'd never been to Sunday school; I had no idea. But I did know that a good mother finds answers for her daughter.

I called Amy's Sunday school teacher. "Hey," I blurted out before we'd even said our hellos, "what comes after rock?"

That teacher cared, not only about Amy, but also about Amy's parents. She was instrumental in bringing me into the Sunday school program. God knew I had empty holes in my life that didn't prepare me for being a parent. He used that willing Sunday school teacher to show me how to fill them up.

Success

North York, Ontario. Rosita knows she's a successful teacher in the eyes of her young teens and in God's eyes, but it's not because the flowers are all that easy to see. She explained, "Those boys never tell me. Not one word about having a wonderful time in Sunday school or what a great teacher I am. They never say thanks. But they do come back every week. Their parents smile at me a lot. Best of all, my boys keep bringing their friends. So, who needs words!" Anyone got a vase for the flowers?

 Flowers From God

A TEACHER IS BORN! SEEDS ARE PLANTED!

*"You can impress people from afar,
but you can only impact lives up close."*

—HOWARD HENDRICKS

❖ 98% of all churches in our country have Sunday school. Approximately 36 million students attend every week. They are taught by about 4.1 million Sunday school teachers.

❖ Where do all these volunteer teachers come from? How does a teacher get born? Every story is different.

Dale: A Teacher Is Born

Toccoa Falls, Georgia. Some volunteers are born teachers. Others discover the gift through a God-directed "accident." Dale's college friends talked her into substitute teaching in their seven-year-olds' Sunday school class. Hey, they're just little kids. Only an hour. How hard could it be? Yeah, right! She took one look at all those kids who weren't looking at her and ran to get Beth, the Sunday school superintendent. Help!

Beth taught the class, and Dale spent the rest of the morning watching. The class interactively studied the plagues, even packing themselves into a closet to experience the plague of darkness. When class ended, Beth figured Dale would escape forever, but instead she announced, "I want to teach—really teach."

"Why?" Beth probed.

"Because Sunday school isn't just sitting and listening like I thought it was. It's fun, and this morning I discovered that God wants me to be part of the fun."

Michael: A Teacher Is Born

Lorton, Virginia. "For years, I was an usher," said Michael. "Then one Sunday I visited the elementary class to tell the children that I was collecting old bikes for needy kids. I got to the class door and instead of going right in, I watched through the window. Everyone was having such a good time.

"The longer I watched the more certain I was that I had to be in that room, where the real God-action is. Ushering is a fine job, but now I've got the best job. I'm a teacher!"

Daniel: A Teacher Is Born

Casper, Wyoming. "I can't teach. I wish I could, but that's not my gift. Never happen!" In the strictest sense, Daniel may be right, but in another he is simply a unique teacher. His job? "I meet every one of the junior boys at the church door when they arrive. I make a big deal over them. I officially escort them to the classroom." The boys love it. "No, I don't have the gift of teaching," said Daniel, "but I can talk and laugh and let them know that they are very special to me, to this church, and to God."

Missy: A Teacher Is Born

Springfield, Oregon. Missy is eighty-seven, and this is the first year she has ever been in an adult Sunday school class. For the last seventy-nine years without a break she's been teaching four year olds.

"One Sunday morning when I was eight," said Missy, "the preschool teacher didn't show up. I substituted, and I've been teaching ever since. When I was twelve, I realized that God had put me on earth for one main reason. I was to teach little children about Him and about His Son. If that was what He wanted of me, then that was what I was going to do."

Imagine the reception Missy is going to get in heaven when she sees the results of her eight decades of faithfulness!

Bill: A Teacher Is Born

Hoffman Estates, Illinois. "You're a scoutmaster. Surely you can handle fifth-grade Sunday schoolers." And that's how Bill became a volunteer.

"I was a new Christian and was worried that I didn't know enough. I started with an easy story—Noah. I knew I had to keep the boys busy, and the Lord knew I needed help. We researched the ark and built a scale papier-mâché model six feet long. We went to a lake to study how a flood affects an area. As I struggled with how to teach the Bible, the Holy Spirit taught those kids through me."

The class asked Bill to move up with them when they went to sixth grade, and he was honored. Now that first class is grown, and four of those boys are spending their lives in full-time Christian service. "There is no way I could have been that good a teacher," Bill said. "The Lord knew I needed the encouragement of success at that early point in my Christian life, and He helped me. I've got a word for new teachers. Don't be overwhelmed. With God's help, you'll never be inadequate."

Vern: A Teacher Is Born

Trout Creek, Ontario. Vern agreed to teach Sunday school because he thought it would be a great way to help kids develop morally and to make right choices. "I believed that if they were good enough," Vern explained, "they would get to know God."

His church's new pastor visited Vern's Sunday school class. After class, the pastor told him, "You have all the skills, and the kids like you. But something is missing. I suspect you don't really know Jesus Christ. Let me explain where the Christian life really begins."

Vern listened and accepted God's salvation offer. "Now, when I teach, I really teach. I've got a relationship with the Person who headed up Sunday school."

BUDS: TEACHING PRESCHOOLERS

"It isn't lowering, bending, stooping, crouching down to children that is so tiring. It's the reaching up . . . Reach up, stretch, stand on our tip-toes."

—JANUSZ KORCZAK, WARSAW, POLAND,
WHO WOULD NOT ABANDON 200 ORPHANS HE LOVED.
(THEY WERE GASSED TOGETHER IN TREBLINKA CONCENTRATION CAMP)

"I love my teacher, Mommy. Can we take her home?"

—TWO-YEAR-OLD JESSICA

"Dear Jesus, please make Daddy stop drinking and be nice to Mommy." Four-year-old Bradford (Ames, Kansas) knew that something was terribly wrong in his abusive family. His parents finally divorced.

Not surprisingly, Bradford is a behavior-disordered child. Yet every few weeks, he'll make a point of getting his teacher, Joann, alone and asking, "God always loves me, doesn't He?"

"I reassure him," Joann said, "but I realize that he'll have to hear this truth over and over again throughout his life in order to know and feel how true God's love is.

God always loves me, doesn't He? Yes, Bradford. He always does. Yes, He does.

Budding flowers in our Sunday school nurseries and preschools! Open your arms wide and collect the buds. Thank you, teachers of the smallest members of our church. Do you have any idea how important you are?

What Jimmy Learned

Littleton, Colorado. "Don't say that!" Jimmy interrupted his teacher, Emily. It was his first time in the Sunday school. She continued teaching and he interrupted again. "Don't say that. Don't say that."

Finally she realized what was wrong. "I stopped the lesson," she said, "and Jimmy and I talked. As he was leaving, I asked, 'What did you learn today, Jimmy?'"

"I learned," said this precious little boy, "that God is not a dirty word."

Bear

Elyria, Ohio. Bear had only one eye and his arm was hanging by a thread, but Hannah loved him. Bear always accompanied her to Sunday school. When her teacher, Janet, suggested the children pray for people who were sick or hurting, Hannah, her arms around poor, tattered Bear, prayed, "Dear Jesus, please make Bear better."

Then Hannah had such a good time in Sunday school that she forgot Bear and left without him. One of the class helpers took Bear home and "healed" him. When Hannah got him back, she beamed. "God fixed Bear!"

Janet agreed with Hannah. "God uses teachers throughout our life journeys to sew our bears together and to help mend our broken lives."

Postcard Pillow

Colorado Springs, Colorado. Jamie missed Sunday school one Sunday, so his teacher, Diane, sent him a postcard. Four year olds don't get much mail. Jamie was thrilled. He didn't even know the postman knew his name! He and the card couldn't be parted. He even slept with it.

When Sunday came, he was back in class. His parents were in church, too, brought back by their son who wouldn't have it any other way. He told them, "I have to be in Sunday school. They need me there."

Major Prayer

Springfield, Ohio. When Doug asked if any of his preschoolers would like to pray, Kyle volunteered. He asked Jesus to take care of his parents, grandparents, Sunday school friends, and every person he could name in the church. His prayer went on and on and on.

While he prayed, his little friends wandered off to play with their toys. For Doug, it was a flower-filled moment. "Kyle and I sat together, hands folded, eyes shut, while that child held his major conversation with Jesus."

FLOWER POWER: TEACHING ELEMENTARY STUDENTS

A bouquet of flowers puts a smile on 100% of the recipients' faces!
—*Study by the Human Development Lab, Rutgers University*

In a cubic foot of snow, there are 18 million individual crystals, and not one of them is like any other. The same is true of the children in our Sunday schools this Sunday. God only makes originals.

Want an easy job for Jesus? This isn't it. Six to ten year olds stretch the minds of thirty-two and fifty-six year olds! I know this from personal experience.

I was telling the story of Jarius' daughter. When Jesus told the mourners that she wasn't really dead but only sleeping, Jeffery asked, "Was she dead or not?" I assured him that she was dead. "So why did Jesus lie?" He wasn't being smart-mouthed. He just wanted to know.

On went the lesson to the point where Jesus raised the little girl. She was immediately alive and healthy. Kati's eyes widened. "Who taught Jesus magic?" she asked. "Who taught Jesus such strong white magic?" In her family, occult concepts were familiar. Somehow God helped me explain the miracle to this girl in words she could understand.

When our answers are smarter than we teachers are, we can know for sure that God has gifted us with flowers. Let's take them home and enjoy them all week.

Only Children

Pennsylvania. Forty years ago a Philadelphia congregation watched as three nine-year-old boys were baptized and joined the church. Not long after, as its membership dwindled, the church sold the building and disbanded.

One of those boys was Dr. Tony Campolo, Christian sociologist at Eastern College, Pennsylvania. "Years later when I was doing research in the archives of our denomination," Tony said, "I decided to look up the church report for the year of my baptism. There was my name and Dick White's. He's now a missionary. Bert Newman, now a professor of theology at an African seminary, was also there. Then I read the church report for 'my' year: *It has not been a good year for our church. We have lost twenty-seven members. Three joined and they were only children.*"

Only children! Give children a few years of Christian nurture and these "only children" will take discipleship to a whole new level.

Not Afraid

Hurst, Texas. Jan teaches six year olds. One Sunday her children were studying God's special care for them, and she asked them to draw a picture of a time when they needed God's care. Andy drew a dark picture of a little boy and girl standing outside a house in the rain. "My mom locked me and my sis out," Andy volunteered. "It was raining something awful. She wouldn't let us in all day. We were scared of the thunder and lightning. Jesus was with me, but I didn't know it then. If I had, I wouldn't have been so scared." He smiled, "I know it now."

Dwayne Picks

Buffalo, New York. Pick! Pick! Pick! Dwayne's fingers never stopped. His nervous habit was ruining the colorful contact paper his teacher had used to cover the Sunday school table. As he picked off each little sticky inch, he'd wad it into a ball.

Rhoda, his teacher, said, "I was furious when I saw how destructive Dwayne had been. But God stopped me before I yelled. He reminded me that Dwayne's parents had separated and shortly afterward his father had been killed. The stress he was under was tremendous, and picking helped him deal with it. Without picking, I don't think he would have been able to listen."

After class, the boy and his teacher recovered the table. Sometimes God's flowers come in the form of extra wisdom, wisdom that allows a teacher to say, "Pick if you need to, Dwayne. God cares and so do I."

Cult Cure

Minneapolis, Minnesota. Eight-year-old Jeffrey and his father were watching a TV program about a cult. The youngster kept saying, "That's not true. That's not true."

"How do you know that's not true?" his dad asked.

"Well," responded the youngster, "When you've been in Sunday school as many years as I have, you know what's right and what's wrong."

Scott's Shell

Trumansburg, New York. Scott's background made him insecure. He trusted no one. For seven months, he came to Sunday school class, but he refused to take off his jacket. It was his protection against the kids, the teachers, and even God. With it on, he wasn't wholly there, he wasn't vulnerable. Like a turtle, he was protected by a cloth shell. His teacher prayed for a miracle.

God delivered. "Last Sunday," his teacher said, "God sent me a huge bouquet. Scott took his coat off. He took his coat off!"

Well, It Worked!

Columbus, Ohio. Jaye started coming to Sunday school and was developing a keen interest in Jesus. His teacher, Cathy, was disappointed when his working mother found it too hard to keep bringing him. Cathy lost contact with the family, but didn't stop praying that God would allow her somehow to connect with mother and son again.

Some time later, she had surgery and was just waking up when she saw a woman she recognized. "I know you," she said.

"No, honey," the nurse responded. "Everyone says that. It's just the anesthesia."

"No, I really do."

Then it hit Cathy. This was Jaye's mother. She blurted out, "I've been praying for you and hoping that I could get to know you."

It wasn't the normal way to bring Jaye and his mother back to church, but who dares say what's normal with God?

Won Two!

Chicago. Audrey, ten-year-old daughter of an alcoholic mother, walked one mile from the housing projects to the church. The women of that church taught her about Jesus, and also about all the basics she wasn't getting at home—the importance of changing her underwear, washing and oiling her hair, wearing deodorant. Changes happened to Audrey and to her mother as the child shared her faith. Her teacher, Sandra, said, "Her mother stopped drinking, came to know Jesus, and was able to move out of public housing. Celebrate the witness of a child."

Daddy Prayed

Remington, Indiana. Beth Ann was told by Tori's father, "I started praying before Tori was born that God would bring the right Sunday school teacher into her life. I have no doubt that you are the person I was praying for."

Family Glue

Boone, North Carolina. Linda's children made Christmas calendars for their parents, each one personalized with the child's photo. She knew that many of her children were from broken homes, and those kids made two calendars.

A divorced father took his daughter's calendar to work. Each day it reminded him of how much he missed his family. He and his former wife are talking again. Only God knows what this child's Sunday school craft project will eventually accomplish.

The Terrible Reader Miracle

Providence, Rhode Island. Joshua always volunteered to read, and he was a terrible reader. "Why," his teacher wondered as he stumbled through the Bible verses, "would he put himself through this?" But about the third time Josh read, she caught the bigger wonder. Not one of his lively, typically rude, teasing, seventh-grade peers ever made fun of him. Instead, when he stumbled, someone would volunteer the word. When he finished, the other guys would smile and nod their approval.

"Some teacher before me had gotten through to these dozen boys," Jessica, said. "That teacher had taught Joshua that God wanted him to read the Bible, even though he stumbled. And that unsung teacher also taught Josh's friends that God expects them to cheer on fellow Christians when they attempt hard things for Him."

WILD FLOWERS: TEACHING TEENS

One-third of all our teens do not know the significance of Easter.

— GEORGE GALLUP JR.

Puck Hog

Hudsonville, Michigan. Mike, an overly aggressive puck hog, was the best hockey player on his church team. But as he bought into the league's goal—to win kids for Christ through the hockey team—his attitude, language, and playing style changed. He was elected youth coach.

His team would have won the championship if Mike had played. But he chose to stay out of the game entirely. He explained, "If I'd taken Brian out and put myself in, he wouldn't have stuck around to hear about Jesus. We really won today, you know. Brian became a Christian."

Youth Outing

London. From Phil's perspective, the whole youth outing was a waste. Not one of his kids was interested in hearing about Jesus. Sulking slightly, he went to the back of the bus to read his Bible on the trip home. "Read out loud," a kid suggested when she saw what he was doing. Amazed, he did, and several others stopped kidding around to listen. For 45 minutes he just read the Bible. The trip ended too soon. "Will you come tomorrow night and read to us?" several asked. So, the next night and the next, they gathered in a coffee shop and just read Scripture. Eventually half those young people became Christians.

Gospel Napkin

Lowisville, Texas. "My sister thinks because you go to church you can tell me all about this Christianity stuff," Tom said to Timothy, one of the youth group guys. He was right. Timothy loved Christ and studied his Bible regularly. The two boys met for breakfast, and Timothy outlined the plan of salvation on a paper napkin. Weeks went by and Tom called again. "Hey, I just wrote my first stuff in my Bible," he said. "It's the date when I became a Christian." To help him remember his commitment, he had taped the napkin up in his room, right above his girlie posters. Christian maturity doesn't happen overnight!

Running Bet

Lynn, Washington. "Bet you can't win," challenged a guy from a church Stacy had never attended. She took his bet. If she lost the race, she would go to youth group for four weeks—no excuses. She practiced hard. "But my feet—and God—had other plans," she said. "I came from a dysfunctional, non-expressive family. The first Sunday I showed up to pay off my bet, people welcomed and hugged me. Even as I told myself how stupid that was and how much I didn't like it, I know I was lying to myself." The four weeks ended, and Stacy kept coming. Happy ending. "Four years later, my love for the people in that church led me to accept the love of Jesus."

Clean Feet

Willowdale, Ontario. The teen class did a foot washing to demonstrate its willingness to serve. Teacher Janet knew it had been great fun, but did it mean anything to them beyond clean feet? "After class," she said, "I discovered that an ice storm had left my car covered with thick sheets of ice. A teen was chipping the ice for me. 'Just being a servant,' she explained. 'You know, like we talked about.'"

First Steps

London. "I was driving my young teen youth group home from a party," Tristan said. "One kid asked, 'Do you read the Bible?' When I said yes, he and his friends said they did too. 'How long do you read?' they asked. I answered, and they all said that was about how long they read too. 'Do you pray? How long?' With every question, these kids told me that they were matching or outdoing me."

Tristan knew these kids weren't Christians, and their prayers were in the don't-let-me-get-caught-and-help-me-quick category. "They thought it was important to talk out what it means to be a Christian. They were using this talking step to move them closer to a spiritual flying leap."

Flowers From God

IN FULL BLOOM: TEACHING ADULTS

> "We loved you so much that we were delighted
> to share with you not only the Gospel of God, but
> our lives as well, because you had become so dear
> to us."
>
> —PAUL TO THE THESSALONIANS

> When people start coming to Sunday school, their
> annual giving rises an average of $1,319 beyond
> what they gave before they started attending.
>
> —CHRISTIANITY TODAY RESEARCH

The adult class in my church was challenged to dedicate $20 that week to Jesus. We should give it to someone simply because that person had a need. I didn't think I'd have anything to report the next Sunday. In my normal workweek I didn't run into needy people.

The temperature dropped to five degrees one evening. On my drive home I saw a woman waiting for a bus and invited her to wait in my warm car. Minutes later a man arrived at the bus stop, stomping his feet and clapping his hands to keep warm. We invited him to join us in the car.

It wasn't until he was climbing into the back seat that we realized he was a street person. "Thanks. If I had any money I'd pay you for this." He proceeded to educate us on how to survive on the street. "I go to church shelters sometimes," he said, "but all Christians are hypocrites."

"Hey," I contradicted. "This is a 'Christian' car!" That brought on more stories about how awful Christians are.

Half an hour later, as the man left to catch the bus, I remembered the assignment. I handed him the $20 bill. "In Jesus' name, be safe." He didn't smile or say thanks; he took the money, shook his head, and walked away.

Sunday I told my story, and so did the other students. Jack had sent his money to a missionary in Japan, labeled it "fun money," and suggested dinner at a restaurant. Jim gave his to a homeless man undergoing cancer treatments. Ralph gave his anonymously to a janitor who was always willing to help. Peggy's went to buy treats for a shut-in's beloved dog. Each of us saw Jesus at work through us that week because a Sunday school teacher dared to challenge us adults to action.

Important Home

Vermillion, South Dakota. Not long ago Christians in China needed to register with the government and many were persecuted. Paul, a first-generation Chinese American, was a pastor with a problem. He couldn't get Chinese people to come to a church to learn about Jesus.

They just couldn't shake the idea that someone would turn them in for attending. So Paul turned his home into a church. "These people feel safer in my home, studying the Bible, coming to know Jesus, and even being baptized. I live in a very important home," he said. "It's a Sunday school classroom, a worship center, and a fellowship area all in one."

Anger

Woodstock, Georgia. Valerie's adult class studied Christian responses to anger. They even wrote appropriate Scriptures on notecards to help them in the weeks ahead. Two months later one member testified, "My very angry friend called me. She was yelling so loud that I'm not sure she needed that phone. I pulled my anger cards from my purse and used them to calm her down. I helped her see the situation through God's eyes. What I'm learning in this adult class is getting spread all over my friends."

Life Saver

Carlsbad, California. Henry tells people that John, his Sunday school teacher, saved his life. Henry's wife joined a cult, divorced him, and took the children. He struggles daily to find a reason to continue. "He calls me in the middle of the night and we cry together," John said. "He pulls me out of the worship service to pray with him."

Henry has told him, "Without you to show me Jesus in action, I'd have killed myself."

"If you think Christian education of adults is easy," John said, "you haven't been involved in the real thing."

A BLOOMIN' LONG WAIT

- ❖ Collectively, Sunday school teachers will give 7,517,000 hours preparing and teaching this week's lesson. Four percent say they receive no thanks or recognition for teaching.
- ❖ When teachers were asked to describe how they felt about teaching Sunday school, their top five words were challenging, exciting, rewarding, fun, love-filled.
- ❖ When teachers were asked to describe what a teacher should be, their top five words were loving, patient, creative, caring and energetic.

*A*fter reading his childhood Sunday school teacher's obituary in his hometown paper, Louis, now a pastor in Sioux City, Iowa, wrote an open letter to that special lady. He read it from the pulpit to his congregation as an affirmation not only to eulogize her ministry, but also to affirm his church's volunteers:

> *I remember the way you broke down and laughed when Joseph's coat of many colors kept falling from the flannelgraph board, leaving poor Joseph practi-*

*cally naked. I remember how you didn't lose your
temper when the Elmer's Glue top came off and the
contents drained into your purse. I remember the way
your face looked happy when we kids sang, "Jesus
Loves Me," really, really loud. Thank you, dear
Sunday school teacher, for slicing great concepts in the
Bible into pieces small enough for even a child to
swallow.*

Sometimes we wait a bloomin' long time for God's
flowers of affirmation. Perhaps the wait makes our dedi-
cation to volunteering even more special to God.

7 Years

Fairfax, Virginia. When Tony was in Nadine's fourth-
grade class, she made each child a missionary card as a
prayer reminder. Recently she visited in Tony's home, and
the now eleventh grader showed her his room. There
hanging above the light fixture was the seven-year-old
missionary card. Nadine said, "I wasn't in the least surprised when Tony told me, 'Know what? I think God is
calling me to be a missionary too.'"

15 Years

Paignton, England. The silly old fool had been Sunday
school superintendent for fifteen years. At least that's how
Gordon described him. "All that time he talked about Christ
and living for Him, and I kept thinking that someday I'd tell
him there was nothing to this Christian stuff.

"As unlikely as it seems, I was in the cinema when God told me differently. His call was so clear that I couldn't ignore it. My life felt turned upside down, and I didn't know where to go. So I went, of course, to the silly old fool who had suddenly become the wisest man I knew, the only one who could tell me about salvation."

23 Years

Dear Pastor:

It's been twenty-three years since my seven-year-old friend Wayne walked with me to Sunday school at your church in Kodiak. There I heard the plan of salvation. I never told my teacher, but I accepted Jesus in her class.

Maybe she questioned what fruit ever came from that motley bunch of Alaskan kids. I wish she could know that the Gospel she shared changed the course of my life. God gave me a heart for Himself that kept me through my teen years and college. Now, God has allowed me, through the Christian publications I work on, to extend His Gospel to multiplied millions around the world.

Thank you, first Sunday school teacher. Thank you for believing that ministering to children is important.

In Christ because of you,
David, Portland, Oregon

No Flowers?

Norma used to cry her eyes out because her teaching seemed to yield no success—no flowers in sight, not even the hint of anything green pushing up through the pavement. But she kept on teaching, working hard on her lessons and even making individualized love cards for each child. "Probably use them for dart practice," she grumbled while she worked on them.

Years later, she ran into one of those boys, and was absolutely astounded when he told her, "You know them bits of paper you made for me? I still got 'em!"

Norma was holding flowers when she said, "God hung on to that boy, and He used my cards as glue!"

Homegrown

Chambersburg, Pennsylvania. A new pastor in town is homegrown, raised in the church he now pastors. His childhood Sunday school teacher told how strange it was to sit under his ministry and remember what he was like as a little boy, and how special she felt because God used her to help train a pastor. "I feel," she said, "like the Chinese teacher who started every class by bowing to his students. When he was questioned about this ritual, he said, 'I bow because I never know who the children I am teaching will be in the future. I want them to know how grateful I am to play a humble part in who they will become.'"

Lifelong Teacher

Fergus Falls, Minnesota. John now has a fulltime ministry here, but his story starts in the church furnace room where his first-grade class met. "I remember the day when what my teacher had been saying about Jesus finally sank in. I even remember the dress she was wearing—it was yellow. Years later I became my teacher's pastor. In her last years, she suffered horribly from rheumatoid arthritis. Yet until the day she died, she continued to encourage me in ministry, instead of the other way around. She was my lifelong teacher.

Retirement Vision

Benton, Arkansas. Robin and her husband are in charge of a children's ministry in a retirement community. The vision started with only three kids who lived with their grandparents, but even though it seemed silly, elderly church members felt strongly that they were to minister to children. "So they prepared by hiring us," Robin said, "and they added six Sunday school classrooms. Now we're bringing children from the surrounding communities where many live like third-world refugees. Instead of ministering only to people their own age, these Christians brought God's newest generation—complete with their noise, hurts, and questions—into their own backyard."

A DOZEN ROSES

Volunteer teachers are diamonds.
   Then again, diamonds are nothing more than
chunks of coal that stuck to their job Sunday after
Sunday after Sunday after . . .

A dozen roses! It's hard to pick the "best" stories. But to me, these twelve are especially wonderful.

First Rose: My Story

It all started with Candice's exasperated yelp, "You did it again. You ran out of time before I got my question asked."

I was a Sunday school teacher of teens on a United States military base in Japan during the Viet Nam war. Their fathers flew; their mothers patched together young bodies. If ever a group needed time for questions, this was it. "Next week," I promised her, "I won't prepare a lesson. We'll start with questions and we'll go until we're done."

I worried all week. I'd always been organized. I studied and planned so I wouldn't make mistakes. I asked "safe" questions in class. I was in control. Yet the more I worried about the next Sunday, the more certain I was that God wanted me to trust Him.

On Sunday I opened class by asking, "So who's first?" Six hands were raised. I pointed to the least dangerous looking kid. "My girlfriend's baby sister died before she was born. Will she go to heaven?" she asked.

Before I could answer, a boy who almost never talked blurted, "My dad flew out this morning. If his plane is hit and he dies, what happens to him? He's not a Christian."

I sent up a help-Lord prayer, and started to interact with those children on their heart level. I allowed Christ to show His strength through weak me.

Second Rose

Georgia. A church that had never had Sunday school called a meeting where Pete, a Christian education leader, was to explain how to start one. He tried to organize those attending. "Why don't teen teachers go over there and children's teachers stay here," Pete suggested. Not one of the twenty-one people moved. These never-before teachers had no idea what age level they could teach. *Help, Lord,* he prayed.

God gave him an idea. "All of you who don't mind sticky knees, stand up." Five stood. "You like preschoolers, don't you?" They grinned and banded together. "Who likes whispers, pet stories, and confidential prayers?" People who liked elementary children identified themselves.

They kept dividing by the characteristics of students, and in a few minutes, every age level had volunteers. A Sunday school was about to be born.

Third Rose

Northern Ireland. Dorothy is a miracle teacher who now works with her church's wee ones. When Robert, a pastor, first met her, she was sitting on her floor. She was obese, and fear of falling kept her on the floor all day long. She called Robert as her last resort after her young son had kicked her and said, "I don't want you here anymore."

On his first visit, she asked if he'd like tea. Then she crawled from the living room into the kitchen to get it.

"Have you noticed that God's love has a way of getting people on their feet?" Robert said. "Through the months, as we talked and prayed, Dorothy began to risk a few steps. Her weight started to come down and her self-esteem went up. Now when she crawls on the floor, it's because she's playing with her very special nursery students."

Fourth Rose

Pennsylvania. Everyone else is quiet; this kid is laughing. He's always a half step behind the rest of the youth group. A girl is crying out her pain; he falls asleep. He's the kid Sunday school teachers and youth leaders label "spiritually impaired," the one who makes them wonder if the Lord really would love him if He knew him the way they do!

He's the kid caught kissing his girlfriend in the back of the choir bus, the one who goes sneaking out with her until all hours of the night, the kid who breaks every rule of the youth group, the church, the entire denomination! This kid makes teachers think homicide, not discipleship.

Human perspectives aside, God wants this kid, and He gets him. In his freshman year of college, he accepts Christ and dedicates his life to full-time youth work.

"Twenty-five years ago I was this kid." Duffy said. "Thanks, Christian adults who stuck with me."

Fifth Rose

Fairbanks. A small church was designing a Christian education wing. Everyone had lots of opinions about the construction. Betsy, however, realized that the young teens hadn't been asked. "I thought they'd want a gym or something else unreasonable for a church our size," she said. "Instead they lobbied for a ramp for Hal because 'he's really old and can't get up the steps. And,' they added, 'we want a big area for potluck dinners.' I explained that those dinners took a lot of time, but they responded, 'We know, but they make us feel like we're a church family. We belong together.'"

Sixth Rose

"You grew up in Oklahoma City! Hey, so did I." Mike was comparing notes with another pastor. "What church did you go to?" Here is the story this pastor told Mike:

I went to the church that loved me. My parents were alcoholics. I'm not sure they cared if I lived or died. I know they didn't care where I was or whether there was food in the house. A neighbor sensed there was something wrong in my house. She said, "Every night at 6:30, there will be an empty chair and a place for you at our dinner table. Come any night you wish. You are part of our family."

She invited me to attend Sunday school. I went and found Jesus Christ. Through my high school years, people from that church bought me jeans and shoes. After graduation a group of men told me that if I wanted to go to college, they would pay my expenses. After college, I knew God wanted me to become a pastor. Those men offered to pay my way through seminary.

Let me sing the praises of the Christians at that church. As a child, as a teen, they were the only people who ever loved me.

Seventh Rose

This is Trudy's story. She's from Topeka, Kansas.

Mom went to take care of Grandma when she had a stroke. That left Dad to feed us kids. A great cook he wasn't. About the time we thought we couldn't eat another Dad meal, my Sunday school teacher showed up with fancy sandwiches, buttered, the crusts removed. She said, "A lot of people are praying for your family." I panicked and thought, "Oh, dear, what have we done wrong?" The only time I prayed was when I was in big trouble.

I learned a lot about prayer from that teacher, and I also learned that God can use fancy sandwiches to show non-Christian families His love.

Eighth Rose

"She wasn't the best Sunday school teacher I ever had," David said, "but she was the most faithful. One leg didn't function quite right, and when she smiled, one side of her face smiled more than the other. But there was nothing one-sided about her faithfulness."

After young David moved on to other classes, that teacher followed his life with her cards: birthday, Christmas, graduation, wedding. His children were born and she expanded her cards to include them. David's daughter Michelle went off to college and the cards followed. Three days after that faithful teacher went to be with the Lord, Michelle received her final card. That teacher spent over $300 a month on cards for her 30 years of students.

Ninth Rose

Elyria, Ohio. Kadie wouldn't stop crying. The louder the thunder roared across the sky, the harder she cried. Over and over, she begged her parents, "Take me to Sunday school! Take me to Sunday school!" When the storm subsided, Kadie explained, "In Sunday school God said He would take care of me. I want to go find Him."

"God can take care of you at home, too."

"But I can see Him in Sunday school." Then her parents understood. Kadie had gotten her first male Sunday school teacher and God mixed up. Kadie's teacher was her human model of a loving Jesus.

Tenth Rose

Surrey, England. In preparation for attending their first "big church," Gill was preparing her four-year-olds. They learned the words of the hymns. They practiced how to be respectful during prayer. Gill said, "I was born with one arm that ends just below my elbow. When I showed my youngsters how to put their hands together when they prayed, I demonstrated by putting my one hand against my elbow, assuming they would realize I would have put it against my other hand if I had one."

The next Sunday during the pastor's prayer, Gill looked around at her children. Sure enough. There was every one of them praying, eyes squeezed shut and one hand sweetly pressed against a bent elbow.

Eleventh Rose

Seattle, Washington. For months after four-year-old Kesha's father died, she never spoke except to answer questions directed at her. One Sunday her teacher, Alicia, happened to be in the ladies room with the little girl. Out of the blue, Kesha said, "I like it here. My daddy died."

Alicia said, "I've been teaching 20 years. During that time I've collected about a dozen bouquets that I will hold forever. This one was a sacred moment. She was saying, 'I trust you.' We knelt right there and talked aloud to God."

Twelfth Rose

Plano, Texas. When Kay thinks Sunday school, she pictures the long hallway in her church. At one end, a daddy comes out of his class. From the other, his little son comes from his. They gallop toward each other. Daddy scoops up his son and asks, "What did you learn in Sunday school today?" The little boy grins and answers, "I learned that God is with me even when I take a nap. What did you learn, Daddy?" Now there's a flower picture that ought to be framed.

ENDANGERED FLOWERS

Teachers' watches on Sunday morning do not go Tick! Tick! Tick!
  They go Precious! Precious! Precious!

Teaching Sunday school is not like a spelling bee, where if you make one error you're out.
  It's more like baseball, where the winning team may actually have lost a third of its games.

Knife

Whitesboro, New York. His father is in prison, his mom's a crack head, and eleven-year-old Travis is a gang member. Every Sunday he makes the lonely, long walk from his home to Valerie's Sunday school class.

One week, he brought a knife that converts into a dagger, just to impress the other kids. Valerie said, "After the lesson on Jesus' care, Travis gave it to me because, with Jesus' support, he felt safe enough without it. I carry it in

Flowers From God

my purse to remind me of the reality of my kids' lives. Travis is leader material—for the gangs or for Jesus."

Aron

Los Angeles. Rick was the guest preacher that Sunday. As he and his wife walked toward the church, a dirty, smelly kid with matted hair got off the church bus and attached himself to the couple. "Do you know," eight-year-old Aron told them, "they have food here, and they share it?"

After Sunday school, Aron walked up to the couple again. "Who are you going to sit with?" he asked. Since Rick was preaching, Aron sat with his wife. When Aron's stomach started making the most awful racket, Rick's wife pulled saltines and mints from her purse. For Aron, it was a feast.

As the couple was leaving, Aron asked, "Hey, are you guys gonna be here next week?"

No, but others from God's family will be. That's what God's people are like, Aron. You can count on us. You can count on Him.

Last Hope

Vacaville, California. Justice was always in trouble. When he stopped coming to youth group, no one was surprised. Then his leader, Leroy, ran into him in a store and invited him back to the church.

"Can't," he said. "I'm under house arrest for extortion. This is as far away from home as I can go."

Leroy asked him how it was going. "No big deal," was

the answer. "I've always been home alone, so nothing's different."

Leroy invited him to come back when he was free to come. He showed up one week when Leroy was home sick. After class the substitute phoned Leroy and yelped, "You would have to invite him back! He's a total disaster! And to top it off," she joked, "I'm not sure I believe you were really all that sick!"

Leroy talked about Justice: "We laugh in exasperation about Justice's behavior and also with joy because he returned. We both know that God is Justice's only hope. If we turn him away, where will he go?"

Killer Kid

Phoenix, Arizona. Timmy's first time in the church nursery was a disaster. He bit, hit, and threw things. When the teacher suggested to his parents that he be tested for a learning disability, they got angry and came venting to Ron, the children's leader. "The last three churches couldn't handle Timmy," they said, "and now you're going to throw him out."

"Wrong!" Ron said. "Timmy is welcome here. We are dedicated to working with and loving every single child. We're with you in this."

Now, several years after that first encounter, Timmy is getting the help he needs. After all, he goes to a church where every teacher knows that Jesus loves all little boys, even those who don't fit the usual pattern.

Phillip

Alaska. Phillip is an eleven-year-old boy who lives with his alcoholic mother. He is the only student in his Sunday school class. As Sherry tells him about Jesus, he stands on a table and unscrews a light bulb. She keeps talking and he screws it in again. Over and over he repeats the process while both of them talk about Jesus' love. He's a bright boy who can't pay attention unless he is moving.

He sat with Sherry in church one Sunday but was so noisy that a woman glared and said, "Why can't you keep him quiet? People are worshiping."

Sherry said, "That woman saw him as my problem because I'm his teacher. Wrong! Phillip lives in an almost empty cabin. The yard is littered with bottles, trash, and magazines picturing naked men and women. Phillip, and all the other children like him, are every Christian's problem."

My Turn

Houston, Texas. Bobby, a foster child living with a church family, had been abused and never spoke. One Sunday the nursery lesson was on Jesus' love. His teacher, Kevin, taped a picture of Jesus on a mirror and had each child come up to the mirror to see himself with Jesus.

It was Bobby's turn, and when another child tried to push him away, Bobby spoke for the first time. "No, it's my turn now. I want to see me with Jesus. Jesus loves me."

PRESSED FLOWERS

I was leading a workshop at a Sunday school convention when a young college student came up to ask if I would autograph *Creative Teaching Methods*, his Christian education textbook that I had authored. As I signed, he gushed, "I'm so glad I got to hear you teach." If he had only stopped there—but on he went. ". . . you know, while you're still alive. I thought you were long gone."

Older teachers! What a gift they—we—are to the church. Of course the gifting works the other way around, too. The hug of a child makes my Sunday. A teen who enjoys having a real conversation with me brightens my week. Even college students who are delighted that old age hasn't felled me give me chuckles and wrinkle lines going the right direction.

I was ten when I got my first really old teacher.

Spindly, skinny Miss Bennett stood up and grinned.

We almost-adolescent girls were appalled. Surely this old lady with her slip hanging a full three inches below her dress could not be our teacher!

But then Miss Bennett began to tell the Bible story.

Most of us had been in Sunday school all our lives. We knew the stories—at least in our heads—but Miss Bennett's storytelling was different. She touched our hearts.

Through her we could hear the soldiers talking around the foot of the cross. She coughed and we could feel the dust and heat. Her eyes turned up toward the cross and suddenly our hearts' eyes could see Jesus hanging there in pain for us. Miss Bennett became a beloved teacher, not because she looked the part, but because she loved Jesus and showed His love to us.

Hugs and Flowers

Fort Worth, Texas. Every time Bonnie meets anyone who has ever been her Sunday school student—quite a number, because she has taught most of her seventy years—she hugs. Every one she teaches is her favorite. She's taught all four of Suzi's children. Each loves her. And, in a very special way, she has taught Suzi and her husband, too. They worked with her when they were new Sunday school teachers. She showed them through her life what it means to show Christ's love to our churches' tiniest people.

Bonnie, this note is from Suzi, but never doubt that it's also a bouquet from Jesus:

Thank you, Bonnie. I've heard other people your age, and quite a bit younger, turn down opportuni-

ties to teach. "I've served my time," they say. Not you. You've found what God wants you to do for Him and you're happily hugging your way through life doing it.

Bonnie, I love you. You are an inspiration to me and to my children. Someday, God willing, Bonnie, I hope I have grandchildren. I pray that they, too, will have the opportunity to be taught and hugged by you.

Hall of Fame

Chicago. Pastor Rob has this to say about teachers: "There should be a Hall of Fame for Sunday school teachers. Without thinking, I can give you handfuls of deserving candidates. I remember the funeral of one long-term teacher. Her students—years and years of her students— filled that church with praise for how she had influenced their lives."

Worthy of Honor

Huntsville, Alabama. Ethel started teaching when her son was six months old. He's fifty-two now. Over the years she's taught the children who are now her doctor and her dentist. Her church nursery is named in her honor. Do the math. If she taught just forty-five Sundays a year, and spent three hours preparing and teaching each of those Sundays, her teaching gift to Jesus is equal to 290 twenty-four-hour days.

No Lock-Ins

Mechanicsville, Virginia. Seventy-year-old Mary expressed her desire to be part of Chris' youth group. The look on his face gave away his dubious feelings. She laughed and explained, "I don't want to play volleyball or try to survive all-night lock-ins. Just give me a list of the kids' prayer needs, and I'll pray for every one of them by name and needs every day of the week. And these kids need on-site grandparents. I'll talk to each one every week to find out how life is going." Welcome to the youth group, Mary.

$1.50 in God's Hands

Albuquerque, New Mexico. Thirty men sat in the adult class and listened to their teacher, Calvin. "Across the street from our church," he said, "people are hungry and homeless. Let's do something about it."

Just one Sunday school class. No money in the budget. But people were hungry. They needed Jesus. So the adults agreed that for four Wednesdays, they would come up with $1.50 for each noon meal hungry people ate. The first week sixty-nine people were fed.

"Four weeks was our plan," said Calvin. "But it wasn't God's plan." The ministry grew into an annual $120,000 budget. "This church once gave me a carnation for being its oldest member. If someone had told me that in the twilight of my years I'd be working with the homeless, I would have thought he was off his rocker. But here I am. This is the most exciting thing I've ever been involved in. Miracles are for today, too."

POLLEN TICKLERS (SOMETIMES YOU JUST GOTTA LAUGH)

Normal people walk through the hardware store looking for stuff for their homes.

Me? I walk through looking for stuff I can use to teach children.

—AMIS FROM MONTGOMERY, ALABAMA

Being an educator and being a pessimist are incompatible.

—JOHN GOODLAD

Bad Monkeys

Ballwin, Missouri. Prayer time ended. "How come we're not praying about the bad monkeys that steal people?" a third grader asked. Puzzled, Karen processed the question. Of course! The week before they had prayed for missionaries who had been kidnapped by guerillas.

Understand Now?

St. Louis, Missouri. Josh, a first grader in Marya's class, explained a Sunday school picture to his friend. "Know what happened?" His friend had no idea, so Josh told him what he had learned in Sunday school. "Well, Jesus got whacked! But wait 'til you hear the rest of the story."

Goliath

British Columbia. "How do you think David was feeling as he faced the giant Goliath?" Nancy asked her class. With complete confidence, a youngster answered, "How scared could he be? He probably saw the video and knew he would win." The rest of the class agreed. Nancy said, "Unpredictable comments like that keep me on my toes and make me anticipate each Sunday."

God Called

Prescott, Arizona. Five-year-old Matthew and his parents were new to church. When the pastor asked everyone to turn to Matthew, the child sat up very straight and looked at his mother in amazement. "Mom," he whispered. "God called my name."

Right Answers

Arlington, Texas. The nursery bathroom is attached to the classroom, so three-year-old Randy could hear his teacher, Cindy, from there. She said, "When I asked a question twice and none of his friends could answer it, Randy just couldn't miss his chance. He came hopping out of the bathroom, his pants down at his ankles, grinning and announcing, "Teacher, I know! I know!"

Senior Sweat

Carrollton, Missouri. Dale teaches elderly people. "Yes, they are old, but there is no way we're going to sit around together and get dusty," he said. "I knew I was successfully challenging them when I overheard an eighty-year-old student grumbling, 'I don't think a body should have to work this hard on Sunday.'"

John 3:16

Prescott, Arizona. The five year old stood proudly to recite her Bible verse: ". . . that whosoever believeth in him should not perish, but have ever *laughing* life." Her teacher didn't correct her because she rather liked the idea of ever laughing life—and suspected Jesus did too.

Lucky Shot

Irwin, Pennsylvania. The preschoolers followed along in their picture books as their teacher, Evelyn, told the story of Adam and Eve. "I came to the part where they felt ashamed because they were naked, so they hid from God. One little girl piped up, 'It's a lucky thing they were behind those bushes when this picture was taken.'"

Just Like Us

Hurst, Texas. To help the children put themselves into the story of Joash, Jan had them use butcher paper to trace around one of the children and color in the life-sized boy king. Jan said, "I could tell by the finished product that they had made the connection. Eight-year-old Joash had a crown on his head and yellow, high-topped Reebok tennis shoes on his feet."

SPECIAL CARE FLOWERS

Children are like flowers. If we do not tend them carefully, they will wilt.

Jerry's Jesus

Gordonville, Pennsylvania. Jerry was born with a rare enzyme deficiency. With his mental and physical handicap, his parents wondered how he would fit into a Sunday school class with his peers. They didn't need to worry. Those boys learned that they, like Jesus, needed to give special care to Jerry. They accepted him. They took turns pushing his wheelchair into the sanctuary. They came to his sixteenth birthday party. Three weeks later they carried his body to the grave.

"Mom," he had once said to his mother, "get me new legs." Today she and his Sunday school friends can picture him walking hand in hand with his Jesus.

Giggle Growth

Knoxville, Tennessee. Kinyata was six when she came to Sunday school. She wouldn't talk or make eye contact.

She'd often roll into a fetal position. The teachers learned that her mother abused her, hitting her with a baseball bat because Kinyata didn't know how to read. They reported the abuse to the authorities, and during the two years that followed, they consistently showed her Jesus' love.

Her teacher, Anne, said, "She was bright, but she needed to learn one-on-one. I started teaching her to read and as she learned, she giggled. Her giggles were signs of growing mental health. Her mother noticed the change too. One Sunday Kinyata ran up to me. 'Guess what!' she said, 'I accepted Jesus, and my mama did too.'"

Sarah's Gift

Mary was unprepared to be taught about giving and sacrifice from a mentally disabled woman, but that's exactly what happened. Every month she taught Sarah and others with similar mental abilities. She said, "As a major in the Salvation Army, I always wear my uniform to teach. One week Sarah came up to me and announced, 'Honey, you must be most awfully poor, because you wear the same dress every time you come. But my Jesus is gonna let me help you out.' With that she handed me a bag that contained her best summer dress."

High Praise

Mesa, Arizona. Joe, a mentally disabled ten year old, sings in his church youth choir—sings quietly and out of sync.

"We did great, didn't we?" he asks the leader, Jill, after every performance.

"In a musical sense," Jill said, "he adds nothing, but in a spiritual sense, this child in a wheelchair, this child whose neck is not strong enough to hold up his head, this special child adds high praise. He knows it; so does God."

When?

Anchorage, Alaska. The class includes three mentally challenged adults with preschooler abilities. One of those special adults, a forty-year-old man, hardly ever says a word, so no one had any idea how he felt about the class. Eileen, the Christian education director, discontinued the class for several weeks to give the teacher a break. Finally the man had waited long enough. He pulled his teacher into the empty room where the class had been, looked her straight in the eye and demanded, "When?"

Not Programs

Fort Worth, Texas. Parents in the church had a baby who was genetically disabled. The doctors assured them that it could never happen again, but their second baby was born the same way.

Keith, one of the church leaders said, "As a congregation we'd gotten used to thinking in broad program-filled strokes about children's ministry. Now suddenly these two children became the catalyst to move us away from just programs to real children. We were mobilized into thinking about the special needs of each and every child."

Prayers changed. Love was shown.

Tears were shed. Ministry happened.

EXOTIC FLOWERS AROUND THE WORLD

So let's go outside, where Jesus is, where the action is—not trying to be privileged insiders, but taking our share of the abuse with Jesus. This "insider world" is not our home.

—FROM HEBREWS 13, THE MESSAGE

China

Dee used Christian holidays to share Jesus with Chinese adults who were learning English. "In our drama of the first Christmas, the three men I selected as kings were getting into the role with all the pomp and power they could portray. But when the first king found he was to bow to baby Jesus, he protested, 'I'm a king. Who is he?' I explained the difference between the heavenly eternal King and an earthly temporal king. Later another student complimented him. 'You were a very good king last night.' With awe and genuine humility, this thirty-two-year-old man replied, 'Oh, no! I'm just a little king. The big king is Jesus.'"

Belgium

Sonia was visiting Belgium from her home in Kent, England. People were giving testimonies, and she sensed that God wanted her to tell about how one of her early Sunday school teachers had influenced her Christian life. "Why bother?" she asked God. "I don't speak Flemish, and it's not worth the effort to have my words translated." But she yielded to God's persistent nudge. After the meeting, a woman told her, "I've been resisting God's call to teach. What difference could my time with little kids possibly make? God answered my question with your testimony."

Colorado to Zimbabwe to South Africa

A Kittridge, Colorado, church believes in passing it on. "We start with our church's once-used Sunday school materials," explained the pastor. "We ship them to our sister church in Zimbabwe. Teachers use them, and when they're finished, they send them to their sister South African church. That third church uses them before sending them to a seminary. There they are placed in the library and used to train pastors and teachers."

Australia

Junior girls were discussing what they could do to reach their New South Wales friends who didn't know Jesus. They decided to hire a bus to pick everyone up for Sunday school. For six months they saved their own money to get a bus. When adults realized what they were doing, they also gave. Over forty children met Christ because their friends cared enough to send a bus.

Philippines

Rhoda was the first person to tell the children in an isolated area of the Philippines that they, as well as adults, could pray to Jesus. The children were amazed and thrilled. "Teach us how. Can we really talk to God now? Can we practice?" Now every day when the church bell rings, these children gather to pray aloud for their own town and for children around the world who don't know about the loving God who is waiting to hear from them.

Jamaica

"No, I don't have a Sunday school story to tell you," Johnny, from Kingston, apologized. "There were nine kids in our family, and we all accepted Christ in Sunday school, but no, I can't think of a good story. Sorry."

Nigeria

Balou, a boy from a Muslim family, came to know Jesus in a Sunday school class. The teacher had bits and pieces of borrowed curriculum, but made the most of every piece, every idea. Balou told his friends, "Come hear. This is great." And they came. They, too, met Christ, and their lives changed. No more speaking back to their parents, no more negative behavior, because it would hurt Jesus.

"What's got into our kids?" parents asked the pastor.

"Come to church and find out," he would say. They came and found the answer was not "what" but "who."

Flowers From God

SUMMER FLOWERS

On average, eighteen Christian volunteers will participate in each of 214,008 vacation Bible schools this summer. More Christian volunteers will minister through VBS than populate the entire state of South Carolina. Stand all the VBS children in a line, and they will stretch from the Atlantic to the Pacific Ocean more than four and a half times.

VBS Prints

Los Angeles. One of the church leaders at Rick's church complained after Vacation Bible School because the children had left their sticky, dirty marks on the freshly painted church walls. He said, "I think we should put frames around those prints. Kids left their fingerprints on our walls, and we pray that our VBS left God's prints on their hearts."

Only One week

Texas. "Remember me?" Laura asked Mike. "I was the girl at camp who wanted to know if it was okay to hate my father." Mike remembered Laura. Ten years earlier at a church camp she had followed him around all week. He learned that her father was an alcoholic who, when he was drunk, beat her mother until she lost consciousness.

"That week," Laura told him, "was the happiest in my whole life. It was the only time in my childhood that I escaped from my father. And that week I became a Christian. Because of that week," she said, "I went to a Christian college. I met and married a Christian man. Together we're building a Christian home."

Such a Little Thing

Philadelphia. Bruce spent the summer after his freshman year sharing Jesus with street kids. Several years later when he was on the same streets talking about Jesus a young man approached him. "Hey, man," he said. "I lost your picture."

Bruce tried to place the tall youth.

"Yeah," the teen continued, "I kept it with me always. But we moved six times. It was the only thing I didn't want to ever lose. I lost your picture, man."

Picture? Picture? Then Bruce remembered that first summer. He was flying back to college and had a layover in Chicago. He'd bought a postcard, and sent it to Robert. On it he had written, "I'm your friend forever."

Stick Around

Williams Bay, Wisconsin. Jason was Steven's favorite second-grade camper and third-grade camper and fourth-grade camper. Year after year the boy came back to the camp, and year after year Steven was his counselor. When

Flowers From God

he was a young teen Jason asked Steven, "Do you remember when I was a little kid? You said Jesus could help me make right choices. Now I'm using what you taught, especially when I decide about sex and drugs. Thanks."

Steven said, "A lot of exciting things happen for Jesus in summer ministries. I had to be involved for five years to hear about this one."

Healing the Hurts

French Camp, Mississippi. When she was a child, Nadine went to a camp for children who had been physically and sexually abused. She said, "I fit. My self-esteem was very, very low, yet those wonderful, God-loving people let me know that I was important to them and to God. They even understood why I couldn't let them hug me.

"I knew then as a young child that I wanted Jesus in my life, but for hurt children like me, that decision does not come easily or quickly. I finally trusted Him enough my senior year in high school to give Him my life."

Prison Bypass

Tabernacle, New Jersey. Carl tells this story: "Al was court committed to our camping program instead of being sent to prison. It doesn't make a totally exciting story just to say he met the Lord at camp and became a role model to the other seventy-five kids who were also in the program. But think about it. Is there a better story? Is there?"

SMELL THE FLOWERS

Teaching requires celebrating the already of God's fulfilled purposes while awaiting the not yet.
—ROBERT PAZMIÑO IN GOD OUR TEACHER

*T*he next time you're discouraged, the lesson didn't work, the kids didn't come, the desperately needed human affirmation wasn't there, take a time out. Sit in a comfortable chair and fill this page with the names of the students God has allowed you to touch. As you write, picture their faces. Ask yourself, what would I tell someone who asked me to explain why I do what I do? How could I explain it with a story one of these names helped me remember?

And when you are finished, take a deep, deep breath. I suspect you just might smell the aroma of flowers from God.

❖

❖

❖

❖

❖

❖

❖

❖

❖

❖

❖

❖

❖

❖

SHARE YOUR FLOWERS

*T*hrough you, God can send flowers to other teachers also. Do you have a story about a time when God sent you flowers because you work for Him, and because He loves you? Would you share that story with me? I'd love to pass it along to teachers who've been waiting to receive flowers from God.

Please send your flower story to:

lefeverm@cookministries.org

or

Marlene LeFever
Cook Communications Ministries
4050 Lee Vance View
Colorado Springs, CO 80918.

Flowers From God